"A very easy read with tons of valuable information. I learned how to fix my Sales process, and I am becoming better at communicating on both sides of the conversation. I recommend that everyone read and learn this amazing new perspective for Sales Training and Business/Personal Communications ASAP!"

Gabriel Flores
President/Chief Executive Officer
We InoV8
Professional Services

The Quarter Method

Sales Training System

Part 1
Psychology of Sales

by

Roy "Will" Wilhite

published by

duffin|creative

austin, texas

The Quarter Method Sales Training System, Part 1: Psychology of Sales
Copyright © 2015 Roy "Will" Wilhite. All Rights Reserved.

Published in the USA by
Duffin Creative
5701 W. Slaughter Ln Bldg A130-205
Austin, TX 78749
Visit us on the Web at duffincreative.com

ISBN-10: 069250365X
ISBN-13: 978-0692503652

Library of Congress Control Number: 2015951035

Printed in the United States of America

Table of Contents

Introduction

(Do not skip this!)

The Quarter Method Sales Training System covers all phases of the sales timeline. This book focuses on the Psychology of Sales, and is the first of a three-part system. In this book we will learn the how and the why of human behavior. We will apply psychological concepts to your understanding of sales and the sales process. In *The Psychology of Sales* we will be mostly focused on the first two phases of the sales timeline: the introductory phase and the getting-to-know-you phase. The next book in the series is *Communicating in HD*, and it focuses on how to communicate. In *Communicating in HD* we will discuss all phases of the sales timeline, how to use both open and closed questions in each phase, and how to transition from one phase to the next. The final book in the series is *Closing Linguistics*, and this is where you learn to close. This is the last book, because if you had not learned the first two key elements—Psychology and Communications—you could *not* apply the concepts in *Closing Linguistics*.

Your task for this book is to start recognizing and then changing bad habits. Some of you may have an innate understanding of the concepts in this system, and if you do, you are a natural communicator. For others, this will be your first exposure to the how and why of sales. This system will teach you to not only sell better, but if you let it, it will change the way you think and the way you communicate. This type of change requires dedication to the training concepts. You must be fully committed to getting better at sales, better at communicating with others, and better at being you.

My educational background is in Psychology and Communications, but my most valuable knowledge and experience came from my PhD from The School of Hard Knocks.

I recently saw a quote that read, *"The difference between school and life: In school, you are taught a lesson and then given a test. In life, you are given a test that teaches you a lesson."*

I thoroughly enjoyed my collegiate learning experiences, but let's be honest: I have to go back and refresh my psychology and communications concepts and lessons, or I will forget them completely. My Hard-Knock lessons have been beaten into me to such a degree that they have become wisdom. The truth is, there is no college for Sales. "Sales Professional" is an on-the-job-learning career. Humans learn by association. All of those collegiate lessons are difficult to associate with for someone with little to no experience, and therefore the lessons do *not* stick. In the Hard-Knock lessons, you were there, you were living through that lesson, and you learned by association and gained wisdom from the experience.

Has anyone ever walked out of a college class with gained wisdom on the course material? Gained wisdom in life…of course, but not in Psych 105. All professionals gain experience and wisdom in real time, through life lessons. *No one graduates as an expert in their field!* I started my sales career when I was 16 years old, and 29 years later I have had major and minor successes and failures. I have had Amazing months, and months when eating was a challenge. But through it all, I persevered. I learned, mostly on my own and usually in a trial-by-firing-squad situation, but I learned. I have had numerous Sales Managers, and I have been the Sales Manager for numerous others, and I understand through experience and wisdom that most Sales Managers are really good at sales, but they have no idea how to teach success. Even worse, most Sales Managers don't think training their team is part of their job.

Here's what I have figured out over the last three decades: your manager is just as worried they are going to lose their job as you are about yours. That fear makes them make bad decisions. Instead of admitting they are not amazing sales trainers, they try to hide their weakness by intimidating the team and setting unrealistic expectations for the team's success. The irony is that in my experience, 95 percent of business owners are just as lost on a day-to-day basis. The business owner is afraid they are going to lose their business.

The owner usually relies on the Sales Manager or the Sales VP to bring in the money and keep the company above water. Two things suffer in this equation: 1. The business. 2. The staff. My advice to those business owners and Sales

Managers is simple: *It is okay to be ignorant, but it is not okay to be stupid.* Ignorance simply means you lack knowledge. If you accept your weaknesses, you can learn what you need to know, or hire someone to strengthen your weaknesses. Stupid means lacking intelligence or common sense; and as the saying goes, ***"You can't fix stupid."***

The point is, you are ultimately responsible for your own failures. If there is little to no training available where you work, then you are responsible for getting yourself trained. If your company offers a comprehensive training program that you don't understand, it is your responsibility to find a program that works for you. When you become #1 in the company and most improved in the same year, the powers-that-be will ask you what you're doing to be so successful. Believe me, I have been there numerous times. Sales is never forgiving, but it will always allow you to try again. So my advice to you is jump in, practice, fail, and persevere. Study every one of your sales to find your strengths and weaknesses. Learn everything you possibly can; everyone is capable of teaching you something, even if it's what *not* to do.

I created The Quarter Method by combining all of my collegiate knowledge and all of my life experiences and focusing them through a training lens. My system will teach you to be amazing! The commitment and the follow-through are the things you must wrestle with to become consistently amazing.

I promise you three things: First, you will fail, and probably a lot. Second, you will become frustrated and doubt yourself and your abilities. Third, if you persevere and follow The Quarter Method Sales Training System, you will succeed and become the Sales Professional you deserve to be! I believe in you, even when you don't.

—*Roy "Will" Wilhite*

What is "The Quarter Method"?

TQM Inc., was founded with the single thought that every decision you make will proceed in black and white steps, or put more simply; we live in a go or no-go reality.

You either made the decision or you didn't, you made the sale or you didn't, you either succeeded or you didn't!

While we recognize there can be numerous influences affecting every decision made, we also realize that when the decision goes against you, it inevitably goes in favor of someone else. This is the nature of business.

By training ourselves to analyze each decision and why the decision is being made, we can learn how to manipulate a vast majority of those numerous influences to make them go in our favor.

Why We Use the Quarter

Imagine if you could have a tool that reminds you to make decisions using your head, and that same tool alerts you when you are making decisions that will get you put out on your tail.

For us, that tool is the US Quarter. President Washington represents the thinking side of the coin, or the "Head"; and the eagle represents the bad decisions of the ill prepared or the "Tail."

The only thing left was to develop the system of training to teach average salespersons to be amazing sales professionals.

Dedication

This book is dedicated to my beautiful wife, my amazing son and my life-long best friend. Without their constant support and understanding I would never have created "The Quarter Method" Sales Training System, let alone finished the three books in this series. They always believed in me, and their faith helped me see the path.

I also proudly thank God for all of the blessings we have received, and for the day-to-day adventure that is God's plan for our family. Life is what you make it through your positive actions and your commitment to faith.

Believe and you will achieve.

Why People Buy
and
How to Influence
Their Decisions

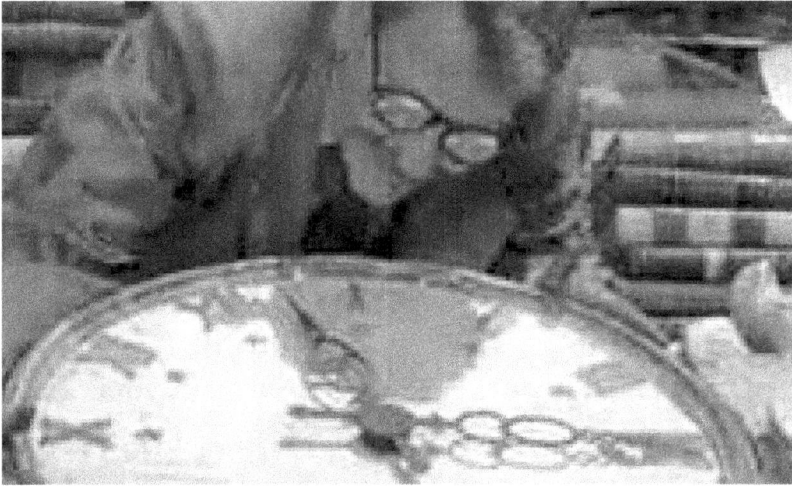

The Current Reality

Looking at your own experiences—How many of you have ever bought a product? More importantly, how many of you like to be "sold"? Being "sold" is a term that has developed a negative connotation associated with being forced to buy something you didn't want. It's like being told you're going to buy something because you aren't smart enough to make the decision without the obnoxious salesperson telling you what to buy. I'm going to guess that no one gets excited about being "sold."

On the other hand, how many of you appreciate being helped when you are trying to make a decision to buy? The vast majority of people prefer to listen to the insight of someone who knows more about the particular product in which they are interested. For example, I would love for someone to tell me the honest difference between a Toyota and a Lexus, but I don't want that person to sell me a car. I simply need help making the decision that is best for me, my family, and my finances.

To be blunt, I don't care at all how my decision is going to affect the salesperson. The salesperson's gain or loss does *not* factor into my decision cycle. In fact, the concept of value is lost on aggressive salespeople. If someone helps me to make an educated decision about the product, I perceive an increase in value, and therefore an increase in what I am willing to pay for the product. If I am buying a product that you have, but not necessarily the product I want, I see the value decrease. If the sale benefits the salesperson more than it benefits me, I should get a great discount. Aggressive salespeople don't understand this fundamental law of value: *Value to me will increase the amount I am willing to pay, and value to the salesperson will decrease the amount I am willing to pay. Simple!*

Let's say we are in a bar. We walk up to the bartender and I order a scotch neat. Instead, the bartender hands me a shot of tequila. I tell the bartender that I am severely allergic to tequila, and he/she says that I have to try this tequila. I tell the bartender that if I drink tequila, I will die. The bartender says I should drink this tequila because it's on special. Barring the possibility of this particular bartender having homicidal tendencies, what is the real problem?

Is it that obvious when a salesperson doesn't care about your wants, desires, and needs? Have you ever been angry with a salesperson who didn't listen? Did you buy from them? Have you ever gone back? They are so focused on themselves that they are **not** listening to the person with the money...aka, the buyer.

In this particular scenario, the bartender was told to push the tequila because the owner bought it at some crazy price way below wholesale, and the owner is making a massive markup on that tequila. However, what are the chances of my coming back to this particular bar?

If the bartender repeated this aggressive "sales" approach all night long, how much business did the owner lose? ***Aggressive sales are bad sales.*** Ignoring the client/buyer is detrimental to your brand. Listening is easy, and will increase value and profit margins. Believe me; I made a career of coming in behind bad or aggressive sales reps and gaining clients for life.

Most of the salespeople you encounter don't care about what you just said. They are going to sell you the thing they get paid the most commission on, not the product you want. If you are that person right now, *stop it!* Everybody recognizes that type of salesperson just as quickly as you do. That type of elitist sales approach is killing your business.

Direct Market Selling, a.k.a. Sales 101

When I was much younger and a lot less experienced, I made a really adventurous and ultimately stupid decision to move to San Diego for a girl. I know... how cliché. Don't judge; we've all done it. So I walked away from my current life and my current success. I sold the first company I ever owned, and I moved to San Diego with the naive assumption that I could easily repeat my success. I actually thought "easily" to myself. The job I had lined up in San Diego turned out to be way too entry level based on my experience, and the owner and I would butt heads constantly. In retrospect, the owner was great and I was the A-hole. In my defense, I was only 20 years old. I had a lot of specialized experience but no real wisdom. Live and learn, I guess.

Anyway, the girl I gave up my whole life for changed her mind about living together, and I was forced to find a place to live and a different job. Talk about starting over! Desperate for some form of regular income, I found myself interviewing for a direct sales position with a company that sold roses. I'm not talking about a florist or a downtown wholesaler; I'm talking about a company that ordered a couple hundred dozen long-stemmed roses from South America every day, and sent out an army of idiots like me to sell them to anyone who would buy. If you are cringing at the thought of running through the streets selling roses, I have two things to say to you. First, I completely understand. I felt the same way when I was 20 years old. Second, get your ego out of the way of your success. I learned, and was taught, more about sales, people, social interaction, Psychology, and Communications from that amazing experience than any three other experiences combined.

Once I got my ego out of the way, I realized I was learning raw sales. I learned, through numerous chains of success and failure, how to read people. I learned how to listen! I learned when to deaf-ear the client and when to smile and nod. I also learned how to sell roses. I quickly became #1 at sales and was "promoted" to being a trainer.

Newbies who went out with me would come back excited to begin their rose-selling careers. Then, almost inevitably, they would go out with one of the other trainers and fail miserably and want to quit. I would take them out again and teach the one thing they forgot when they were with the other trainer: <u>I taught them to have fun!</u>

Listen, I was great at selling roses. So great, in fact, that the wholesaler should have changed the name of the flower from "roses" to "Wills." (I'm just kidding. Who'd want to buy a dozen Wills? One of me is more than enough, I promise.) The reason I was great at selling roses was simple: I always had fun! I messed with people, I clowned people, I challenged people's finances, and I really only had one goal walking in the door: make the people smile and laugh!

I know, a lot of you reading this are thinking that I should have focused on the numbers... but that's what the other trainers were doing. **<u>When you focus on the numbers, you are not personable, you are not concerned with something</u>**

**as insignificant as the client's needs,** and you are probably closing less than 10 percent.

When I got past my own ego, I realized that people didn't buy dozens of roses from me because they needed roses; they bought the roses from and because of me. They bought dozens of roses because of our interactions. I would brighten up their day and make them laugh, and they would thank me by buying roses. One of the newbies I took out for a second day of training was completely "negged out" (a term used in some sales circles to describe someone who has let the negatives overcome their attitude). His ego was blocking him like Mt. Everest blocks its would-be climbers.

At our first stop, we packaged up six dozen roses and I sent him (alone) on his less-than-merry way. I stayed at the car making more boxes of beautiful Columbian long-stem Velveteen Roses. I had finished about 10 dozen when he came back with all of his six dozen. He looked like Santa had stolen his Christmas. He said he had been up and down both sides of the street and hadn't sold any roses because the area was bad.

Apparently this particular commercial street was a favorite for direct sellers. To me, that meant they never bought anything and they all had money.

I grabbed my roses and told him to follow me. At the first door, he warned me that we should not go in because the guy inside yelled at him and said he was calling the cops. (Yes, we had the proper licenses...I think.) In the door I go; and as warned, the owner of the business comes stomping to the front desk yelling, to which I abruptly cut him off with one simple question:

"Why are you yelling at me? I don't even know you."

The owner says, "Because you guys come in here all the time selling your $*@# and I'm sick of it."

I nod understandingly and say, "That must be frustrating."

The owner agrees that it is in fact frustrating, and I ask him if he's ever seen me before, and he says no. (Now he's mine.) I say, "Since you've never met me before, is it safe to assume you treat other people walking into the door differently?" He says that he treats clients differently, and I say (rather exuberantly), "The only difference here is that you didn't know you were going to meet me and become one of my best clients."

So I pull out my phone, and I call the number on the card on the desk and ask for the owner. He immediately starts laughing and asks what I am doing, and I say I am setting an appointment for five minutes ago. Then he says, "What are you selling?" I tell him we are selling dozens of beautiful, Columbian long-stem Velveteen Roses at wholesale prices direct to the public, and I add that, with his attitude, he should probably buy all of them to apologize to his staff, his wife, his mother, and his girlfriend. He laughs and says I'm probably right.

I hand him three boxes of roses, and he places them on the counter and opens them. This witty banter goes on for a few more minutes, and he buys 10 dozen with a tip for me and my friend. Three hundred dollars richer, I give him my card and tell him if he ever needs roses to call me. Then I tell him that if he sees anyone else selling roses, he should make them earn it.

We leave, and the newbie is amazed. I repeat this process at every door, and we sell out 30 dozen by noon and go to the beach. Total profit for the day: $900.00 in three hours. Then I explained to the newbie that there is no such thing as a bad territory—only bad attitudes.

This particular direct sales company had an acronym they chanted all of the time. The term was JUICE, and it stood for Join Us In Creating Excitement.

Attitude is infectious! If I start out my day distracted or weak,—or even worse, scared—I will push those emotions to the people I'm trying to sell to. If I'm inexplicably excited and happy, people will want me around. In sales, your energy is everything; it's the reason rookies always do so well out of the gate, but fall apart when they learn "how to sell." Always be excited!

After that profound lesson in "Making Money 101," the newbie was no longer negged out, and over the next few months he went on to become a trainer and eventually an owner. Sales isn't about the numbers; it's about the smiles. The numbers are a by-product of a happy client.

You Understand the Problem. How Do You Fix It?

The first thing you need to do is learn how to ask questions. The only thing you know for certain when you meet with anyone is your product. What do you know about the client, the client's needs, the client's finances, the client's buying cycle, or the client's anything? The answer is *nothing*! Do you think this information is valuable? What if this is a referral from a friend of yours, and they know everything about the company. What do you know? The answer is still *nothing*! How do you get the information you need, and make the client increase their perception of value? ***You ask questions.***

Closed questions

For a professional, there are only two types of questions: open questions and closed questions. An open question forces the client to give you more information or more details about a specific topic. A closed question leads to a one-word response like "Yes" or "No." A trained sales professional only asks a closed question when they already know the response and they want the client to reaffirm it for psychological reasons. The closed question is the bread and butter of a closer because it gets the client to affirm or reaffirm specific thoughts, emotions, or realities. Closed questions start with Can, Are, Does, Would, Have, Is, and May. (For easy recall, just think of the acronym CAD WHIM. A cad is an ill-bred person, and a whim is a sudden desire or change of mind. If you are using a closed question at the wrong time, you are acting like a CAD, and you may be dismissed on a WHIM. CAD WHIM!)

CAD WHIM
Can, Are, Does, Would, Have, Is, and May

For most people, the buying process is stressful even in the best of environments. Money is changing hands, contracts are being signed, relationships are developing, trust is being laid bare, and commitment is becoming a reality. A closer asks closed questions to get the client comfortably down the path. Closers gently nudge and caress the client's subconscious to associate those stressful emotions with peace and acceptance, and then with the excitement and joy associated with catharsis. *(Catharsis: the process of releasing, and thereby providing relief from, strong or repressed emotions.)*

Open-Ended Questions

Open-ended questions, on the other hand, are the bread and butter of all professional salespeople. Open-ended questions get answers. For a professional salesperson, these answers lead to more specific answers or, if used properly, they will lead to any and all future objections. By finding and addressing the objections early, a sales professional can effectively eliminate objections from the close and, more importantly, relieve client stress and build trust and perception of value almost immediately.

Open questions start with Who, What, Where, When, Why and How. 5Ws and an H. learn to use open questions, and your closing percentages will go up dramatically. More importantly, your referrals and repeat business will increase dramatically as well.

5Ws and an H
WHO
WHAT
WHERE
WHEN
WHY
&
HOW

This concept of asking questions and actively listening to the answer is relatively simple to learn, but mastering it is more challenging. I advise a philosophical quote from Epictetus: "You have two eyes, two ears, and one mouth, and they should be used in proportion." Practically speaking, you should be visually focused on your client while actively listening to their answers and speaking just enough to ask your client another targeted question. Taking notes about specific needs, wants, and concerns is always recommended; just remember to maintain visual focus predominantly on the client.

Professional salespeople ask very specific questions to get an understanding of the client. Here is a list of common questions you will probably need the answers to if you want to get the majority of your deals. This is by no means all-encompassing, and you will realistically need to identify the specific questions that will make you a better sales professional for your industry.

• Who will be making the final decision when the time comes?

• If everything goes the way you would like, what would the final deal look like?

• What is your expected time frame?

• What is your company's buying process?

• What is the authorized budget for this purchase?

• What can I do to help your process?

• What specific needs are you trying to satisfy?

• What special wants would you like to consider adding?

• What did you love about your previous vendor?

• Why aren't you using your current vendor this time?

• What do you think will play a bigger role in the approval, quality, cost, or service, and why?

• How would you like the financials to work?

If you haven't been asking questions like these, why? If you don't ask open questions like these, I would be shocked if you close more than 20 percent of the time. That is not an attack against people closing less than 20 percent, but in almost 30 years of sales at every level, I can say my experiences have proven that salespeople who are aggressive, unskilled, or elitist usually have very low closing percentages. That is not to say they don't get paid. Aggressive salespeople are usually among the hardest workers, and what they lack in closing or sales skills, they generally make up for in sheer numbers. Imagine what they could do if they learned to be professional salespeople. ***Imagine the referrals they could earn if their clients actually trusted them.***

Notes

Introductory Phase

Getting-to-Know-You Phase

Advisory Phase

Closing Phase

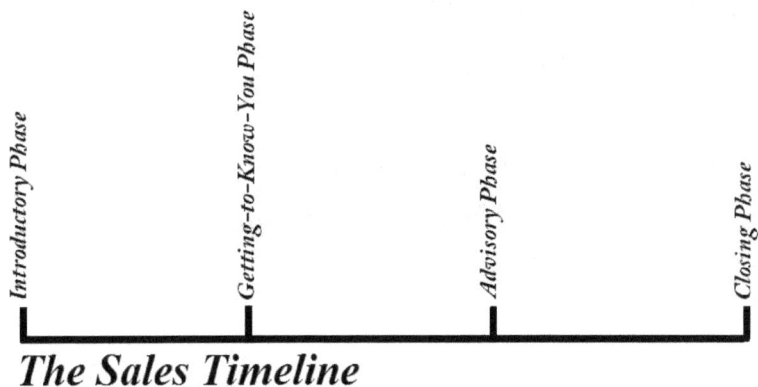

The Sales Timeline

The Sales Timeline

As for the use of the closed question, it is important TO understand that all sales follow a basic "timeline." First is the introduction phase, followed by the getting-to-know-you phase, which is followed by the advisory phase, and then the closing phase. You should completely avoid closed questions during the introductory phase and the getting-to-know-you phase. During the advisory phase, you should only use closed questions strategically, to guide the client into the closing phase and, tactically, to maintain control of the sale. As previously stated, closed questions are the bread and butter of a sales professional during the closing phase. Understanding the sales timeline is intrinsic to both the sales process and closing the sale. These topics are covered in depth in *The Quarter Method, Book 2: Communicating in*

High Definition and in *The Quarter Method, Book 3: Closing Linguistics.* For the purposes of this book, it is important for you to be aware of the timeline because this part of your sales process allows you to comfortably work with your clients from open to close. If you skip following the timeline, you will skip closing the opportunity.

Let's Assume Nothing!

Can you guess what the biggest mistake any salesperson can make is? The answer is "assuming." *Never* assume you know more about the client than the client knows about themselves. It seems ridiculous to even think that salespeople could be making this monumentally egregious mistake, but this is actually happening every day and in a majority of sales. The sales rep thinks that since they know the product and all of its detailed applications, they are the expert to be listened to during the sales meeting. This thought process is so wrong, it's tragic. Let me explain.

A very long time ago, I use to make this same mistake. I use to think that because of my expertise, I had the opinion that mattered. I learned very quickly how wrong I was. What I found out was that although I am supposed to be the product expert, no one cares about my opinion. I had to learn how to get the client to have my opinion. Because the truth is, the only thing that matters is the client's opinion. Right or wrong, they are the buyer; they are the client. I learned to ask questions...lots of questions. Then I learned how to listen to what the client was saying, and what they were <u>not</u> saying. When I finally learned to recognize what wasn't being said, I learned to focus my questions toward the things the clients were avoiding. Eventually the client will reveal the truth, and that's when you get the true objections and the true obstacles.

This process of asking the right questions at the right time will not only give you a precise understanding of the client's needs and fears, but it will also increase both the client's perception of value and the client's trust of you and the brand you represent. Without these essential milestones, the client will be very difficult to satisfy, and most probably, you will either lose the client entirely or you will sacrifice your profit just to stay in the game.

This is the biggest reason most sales people fail: they don't ask open-ended questions, they don't understand the client, and they make stupid decisions due to their ignorance. With no real understanding of the client or the solutions needed to satisfy the client, the salesperson will start to sense their exit, and the fear of losing yet another deal will cascade into desperation. Fear and desperation are, psychologically speaking, very powerful motivating factors. Unfortunately, these strong psychological emotions are not generally associated with good judgment.

Learning to change your psychology to become an effective communicator is a time-consuming endeavor. The best way to accomplish this goal is to consciously practice asking open-ended questions as often as possible; that means all day, every day. In a relatively short amount of time you will notice that you have started to incorporate open-ended questions into your normal daily speech patterns, and from there you will be able to learn when to ask the right questions for most situations.

You will start to subconsciously recognize when people are not being entirely forthcoming or truthful, and with focused practice you will begin to consciously be aware of the numerous but subtle indicators you will need to guide a conversation and therefore a sale. This is the psychological process necessary to become a skilled communicator; I will discuss this in further detail in *The Quarter Method, Book 2: Communicating in High Definition.*

How Do You Know?

• Have you ever been in a multiple-bid process?

• Have you ever submitted a bid and later found out that the company was just using you to satisfy a bid quota?

• Have you ever spent time on a bid to negotiate the best deal possible, and then found out that the company was going to use the owner's relative the whole time, and they were just using your bid to negotiate a better deal?

These manipulations happen every day, and on both sides of the fence. When you get better at asking questions

25

and actively listening to the client, these manipulations will happen to you less frequently. The reason for this is because you will get better at getting to the truth during the first appointment. You will identify these little games and time wasters, and you will address them directly. You will know when it's time to say "thank you" and leave.

Psychologically, it is important for you to learn how to consciously identify when a potential client is a waste of your time and resources. The best way to do that is to develop a system that intentionally shines a light on things the potential client is trying to keep hidden in the dark. By asking open-ended questions as part of your sales process you will be able to uncover most deceptions. Adding questions to your process that are designed to get specific information is crucial. Here are some examples:

1. How many bids are you accepting?
2. Who is the current front-runner and why?
3. Why aren't you using your current vendor?
4. What is your expected timeframe for this purchase?
5. How long do you expect this project to take?

These questions and others like them will quickly uncover time wasters and bid chasers. Developing trust and relationships is the best way to get information about a relative in the bidding process, and experience is the best way to develop the wisdom needed to handle all of these situations. Always be professional and the business, and referrals will come. Always be a sales professional, and you will close a much higher percentage of your opportunities.

I Wonder If I Can Help?!?

If you sell cars, and I walk onto the lot, is it safe to assume I want to buy a car? *No!* It's not even safe to assume that I want to buy a vehicle. I could be a salesperson, or the owner's nephew, or just some guy looking at cars. Assuming that I am there to buy a car is a rookie mistake. Don't be a rookie. It is just as easy to ask me open questions to get to the truth. Maybe I am looking for a new vehicle, but do you know which one? Asking open questions will get you to that answer, and asking closed questions will get you shut down. What you should immediately ask yourself is, "I wonder if I can help?"

One of my favorite rookie sales openers is, "Do you mind if I ask you a question?" I immediately recognize this as a rookie salesperson trying to do what they were told, but not understanding the *how* behind the *what*. This is a closed question; I could just say, "Yes, I mind." However, I tend to have more fun with the rookie and try to teach them something at the same time. When I hear, "May I ask you a question?" I respond with, "You just did," and I keep walking. If they are smart enough, they will realize

I am telling them their opener was horrible because it led straight into a dead end.

Just learning to ask questions is not enough. You must learn to ask questions that interest the buyer. You must learn to ask intriguing open-ended questions. Someone selling hand cream at a mall kiosk may start with something off the wall like, "Excuse me, what was the theme of your prom?" When the client stops to answer this off-the-wall question the sales person could follow with, "What was your skin like back then?" Start with intrigue, begin the transition with something reminiscent, continue with a witty response or a thoughtful musing, and finish with a product demonstration. Simple!

This is the memorable experience the client is looking for at a mall kiosk: quick, amusing, and beneficial. In contrast, "May I rub cream on you?" is off-putting on so many levels its disturbing. The trick is to remember that Sales is a service industry and the sales person's job is to create a positive experience and make sales. You can't help the client if they are running away from you. I will discuss this in further detail in *The Quarter Method, Book 3: Closing Linguistics.*

Notes

I Know What a Closer Does, But What's an Opener?

If the client was opened properly, and all of the essentials were discovered, closing is a simple psychological process of closed agreement questions and a signature. If the client was "rookied" (I just made that up) the entire process is going to be an uphill battle, and you will need your best closer to save the deal. Rookies always think they have the deal. But if that were true, they wouldn't need to use the closer to get the signature. Rookies push their wants on the client, and the closer generally has to start over to correct the deal to reflect the client's needs, wants, and desires. Once the deal is closed, the rookie wonders why he has to use the closer in the first place. ***Don't be a rookie!***

Open Questions Open Doors... Closed Questions May Close the Deal or the Door!

<u>Proceed With Caution!</u>

We've discussed the need for both types of questions and why you should never assume, but what answers are we trying to get out of the client with all of these questions? What are the essentials we need to discover? Essentials are a relatively simple concept. They are Wants, Needs, Desires, Objections, Obstacles, Personality, Decision Maker, and Signing Authority. Some of these can be answered very easily with a direct open question. "Who will be the final decision maker for this purchase?"

Be aware, the answer may not be the whole truth. Have you ever dealt with an office manager who thought they were the final say on everything? If someone says they are the final decision maker, I usually follow with, "So if you decide to go ahead with the deal today, you would sign the agreement and the check?" Most of the time, their answer will tell you who the final decision maker and the signer really are. It is extremely rare for an office manager to have contract authority. By extremely rare, I mean 1 in 100,000, and I'm probably being generous. The one solid exception to this rule is if the office manager is married to the boss. In these exceptions, the office manager is also a co-owner, and he or she may have final authority. This could also be an obstacle you need to overcome. Remember, the concept is easy, but it takes years to master the application.

I will discuss the sales process in further detail in *The Quarter Method, Book 2: Communicating in High Definition* and in *The Quarter Method, Book 3: Closing Linguistics.* The purpose of *The Quarter Method, Book 1: The Psychology of Sales* is to make you aware of the psychological changes you will need to make to be an effective Sales Professional. Put simply, this book is designed to teach the conceptual aspects of The Quarter Method. Books 2 and 3 are designed to teach the practical applications of Sales. Without a strong understanding of the concepts, you will have difficulty associating the practical information in the other two books.

The Truth is Obvious!

If you are assuming that you know the client's needs, and you are losing deals, it is important to truly understand the numbers. Let's say you are an above-average assumptive opener, and your closing percentage is 15 to 20 percent. (In reality, this type of salesperson is usually around 10 percent.) Twenty percent closed means 80 percent lost. Since about 20–25 percent of all sales are purely motivated by price; we'll call those neutral. That gives you a 60 percent loss rate, or 60 percent of the clients you had an opportunity to sell to, bought from your competitor because you didn't listen and ask questions. How much more money would you have in the bank with an additional 60 percent of your potential clients closed? That awareness is essential for you to understand why you should stop with the elitist, assumptive sales process. Not because I said so, but because you like money, and your giving it away every month. Rookie!

I love the psychology associated with lost deals, and how rookies avoid the truth. If you closed 10 percent, you lost 90 percent. Right? But what does "lost" mean? Rookies believe that since the client didn't buy from them, they didn't buy. But what is the truth? Did the client's needs go away because you're a rookie? Of course not! They simply bought from someone else. This denial psychology is apparent when you look at the rookie's pipeline and see the same 25 companies being moved forward every month. When you ask about a particular lost client, they will give you some song and dance about how hard they are working to get back in the door, but the client told them to call back in six months to a year, as if the client decided to hold off their business needs for the next six months to a year. Don't be a rookie.

Notes

Notes

I Want You to Hit Me
as Hard as You Can.

Remember, it is the salesperson's job to sell. It is not the client's job to buy. If you as the salesperson didn't get the deal, you failed. If you are prospecting and you can't get in the door, you failed. If you are making calls and you can't get the potential client on the phone, you failed. If you get the client on the phone but can't get an appointment, you failed.

If the client doesn't show for your scheduled appointment, you failed. It is NOT the client's fault you can't do your job; it's yours. If you are failing, get better. I constantly hear rookies say that the client didn't buy. I make them finish the sentence. I make them say, "They didn't buy from me." Because the reality is, they did buy...just not from you. Own it! Once you accept that you need to improve, you can improve. **Denial is the most expensive mistake you can make!**

When is it OK to Walk Away?

If you lost the deal, *you* lost the deal! If you lost the deal for an acceptable reason, you're doing great. If you lost the deal for an unacceptable reason, *you* failed. All of the things we've already discussed are the unacceptable reasons for losing a deal. What are acceptable reasons for losing a deal? I hinted at the answer to this already, but if you missed it, I said that approximately 25 percent of your potential clients are price buyers. Price buyers are like leeches. They will bleed all of the profit out of a deal and then buy from a website with no service or overhead just to save a dollar. They have no loyalty, and they are generally not worth your time. If you are closing more than 80 percent of your deals, your price is too low. I would seriously question how much profit you have in your deals if you can compete with the Internet wholesalers in your industry.

If There Is No Money In The Deal... There Is No Deal!

What Can I Do for You?

Service-driven sales never focus on price. If you want to make money, you need to focus on service, relationship, and perceived value. I would go as far as to say you should be branding yourself with a consultative sales system. ***I consult with my clients, and when we have figured out the essentials, I facilitate the purchase.*** I prefer for my clients to think of me as a specialist consultant as opposed to a salesperson. I do *not* sell retail, and although there may be more people selling the same product, I am the only one selling *me*. My experience, knowledge, wisdom, and expertise are only available through me. There is a very distinct value to what I bring to the table, and that perceived value allows me to make a profit.

A Little Self-Correction is in Order.

If you are not making enough money, and if you are not making enough sales, the problem is obvious. The problem is you! Once you allow yourself to see the true problem, you can focus on the correction. Every time I lose a potential client, I reflect back on the process and try to figure out where I failed. Usually it's obvious when you lost; sometimes it's not. If you don't know where you went wrong, figure it out. Maybe you need to change your approach. Maybe you need to change your appearance. Maybe you need to change everything. If you constantly lose people from one stage of the pipeline to the next, the problem was during the last phase.

The phases of a pipeline are

1. All leads

2. Contacted leads

3. Identified need for service

4. Schedule appointment

5. Meet with the client

6. Bid/Proposal process

7. Signed Agreement

8. Servicing and referrals

If you are constantly losing potential clients at Stage 3, you need to address the questions you ask on the phone, or at least how you ask the questions on the phone. If you are losing the potential clients at Stage 6, your price is higher than the potential client's perceived value. You need to improve your consulting questions and listen to the client more. If you are losing the potential clients at Stage 2, you need to improve your elevator pitch and the questions you ask during prospecting.

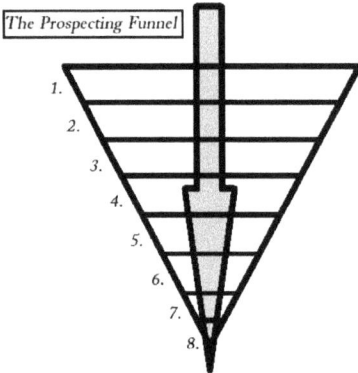

The Prospecting Funnel	The Phases of a Sales Pipeline Are
1.	1. All Leads
2.	2. Contacted Leads
3.	3. Identified Need for Product or Service
4.	4. Schedule Appointment
5.	5. Meet With the Client
6.	6. Bid/Proposal Process
7.	7. Signed Agreement
8.	8. Servicing and Referrals

I will discuss the practical aspects of the sales process in further detail in *The Quarter Method, Book 2: Communicating in High Definition* and in *The Quarter Method, Book 3: Closing Linguistics.*

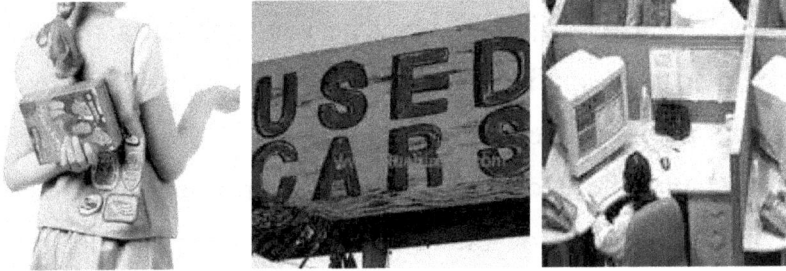

Where Did You Learn to Sell?

This is not rocket science, but without an intentional system in place, how can you correct your unintentional system? *All sales follow a system!* Just because you are not cognizant of your system doesn't mean you aren't using a system. In fact, you probably use the exact same process for each client and don't even realize it. More than likely, you are making the same mistakes with every client, and when YOU fail, you blame the client. If you don't bother to identify the area(s) needing improvement, you can expect the same success you are currently experiencing.

Human beings learn by association. The irony to sales is that most people's experience with salespeople is learned by exposure to the bottom 10 percent of salespeople.

Think about it. Where did you learn to sell? Personal life experiences were first. Then maybe you received a crash course at a retail job, and maybe you attained a position selling cars or appliances or vacuum cleaners, or going door to door for your school or scout group. Few of us are ever truly taught how to sell. I call this the circular sales training reality. How many of you were told to go out and get leads by prospecting, and when you asked how to prospect, you were told to go get leads? I have worked for a lot of companies in the last two and a half decades, and the best prospecting training I ever received was from a manager who said go door to door and get a business card; on the back, write in pertinent information; and tomorrow you will call all of the cards and set appointments.

(I said it was the best training I received. I did not say it was good training. There is so much missing from this "training." Where do I go? What do I say? What is the pertinent information? What is a realistic number of cards to collect? And so on. I have created a training program specific to prospecting and pipeline development, and everyone on my team goes through all of the TQM training programs when they start working with us. On top of that, we do 30 minutes of sales training every morning.)

Obviously, I teach my people everything, and we practice sales techniques everyday in the office, but most sales reps were never trained properly. So you watch what they do and think that must be how to do sales, and that is what you do. The irony is that you can't stand being sold to, but if you have to sell something, that's exactly what you're going to do. It's the only way you've ever been taught, and it's wrong.

You learned that you don't like predatory sales or predatory salespeople. But you honestly believe all sales are predatory. *Sales professionals do not use predatory sales methods.* Sales professionals consult and facilitate. Sales professionals work with clients, not accounts. Finally, sales professionals satisfy client needs; they don't count deals. The starting psychology matters if you want to have long-term success and a very rewarding career.

Notes

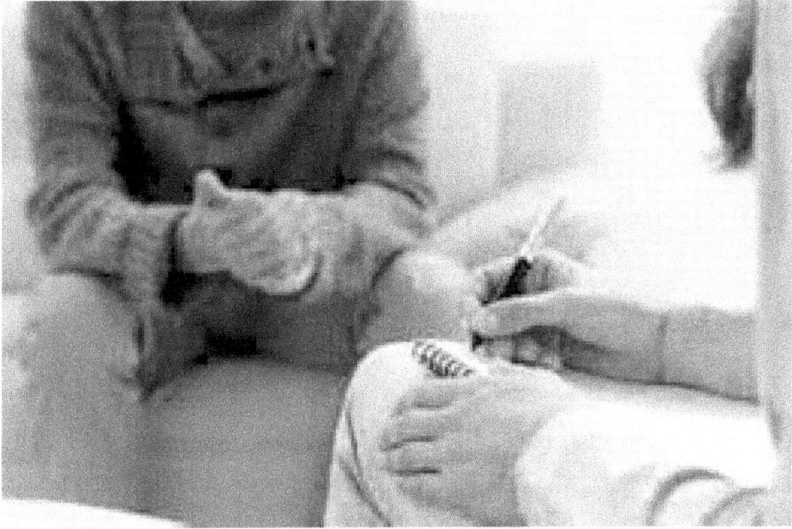

Psychological Application Ahead

There is a psychology technique designed to get the client to keep speaking. The simple version is to repeat the last word the client used, but in the form of a question.

Client: I'm feeling very angry.
Therapist: Angry?
Client: Yes, my family blah blah blah.

This technique gets the client to continue speaking, but in further detail. Psychologists use this to get to the root of the problem. Sales professionals use it to discover the objections. Aside from the obvious benefit of gathering information, this technique also allows you to maintain control of the sale!

Sales Professional: How may I help you today?

Client: I'm looking to replace my old service.

Sales Professional: Your old service?

Client: Yes, I haven't been very satisfied with the service, and the price just keeps going up.

Sales Professional: The price keeps going up?

Client: Yes, I have not had one month where the price didn't increase.

This scenario is an example of a typical conversation with a potential client. If you were this sales professional, would you already start to see the trend? Note that this potential client didn't say they couldn't afford the price increases, and they continued to pay the steady increase. What was their main issue? They were not satisfied with the service. Bad service lowered the perception of value, and now the client is looking for a new service provider.

How many of you keyed in on the price argument as the solution for this client? If you did, you are a wholesaler, and you are doing sales wrong. What if I gave this client phenomenal service and I cost 10 percent more than they are currently paying, but I can lock in the rate at that cost for one year? Do you think the client would sign? Of course they would. I satisfied the primary concern (phenomenal service) and the secondary concern (fixed cost). Price was never an issue. The client gets everything they want, and you get to feed your family. That is a definite win/win!

"The Sales Therapist"

Sometimes during the course of your day you will be called upon to act as a Sales Therapist. (I just made that up, but I bet someone is using it for marketing or as a position title within 12 months.) The Sales Therapist's job is to make people comfortable with a purchase they have already made, and if possible to up-sell to make the client happy. That's right: allow them to spend more money to make them happy.

There was a time when I was a general manager of a fitness center in Los Angeles. This particular fitness center had just been bought from a less-than-successful owner, and there were all kinds of things to correct over time. One of the biggest corrections we made was valuing the membership to an acceptable level to stay in business. The previous owner had been so desperate to make sales, they were giving away memberships for as low as $9 per month. Our correction was necessary to update the club and to maintain current membership's numbers. Members who were currently paying less than $29 per month *would be raised to $29 per month, and new members were signing up at $49–$69 per month. The fitness center starts to turn around, the sales department I trained is closing between 15–17 new memberships per day, and we now offer in-house personal training. All is going well.*

In comes a lady in a business suit. She is visually upset and threatening to sue the new owners. It turns out she is an attorney, and she just noticed that her membership was increased to $29 without her permission. (Letters were mailed and went unopened.) She is actually yelling at the front desk when I come up and introduce myself with a smile. She is angry over the membership increase, she is angry that she is being billed for a membership she doesn't need or use— outwardly, she is angry. If that is all I saw or heard, I would have simply cancelled her membership. (Yes, it is that easy, no matter what your fitness center says.)

Instead, I heard what she wanted to say. I listened for what she wasn't willing to admit out loud, and I was inspired to fulfill our end of the *contract. After she vented for a while, I started asking her questions. (Like a therapist, hence the "Sales Therapist" title.) Why did you sign up in the first place? To get back in shape. How many times have you been here in the last six months? I don't know. Let's go look it up. Two times in six months. Did you buy a membership just to give us money every month? If so, let me be the first to say thank you. <u>She laughs</u> and says no, she is just too busy. Has your life changed since you signed up? No. Have you seen the changes we have made? No. Would you like to? Yes, but I'm still cancelling. Okay, follow me.*

We go through the tour and I remind her of all the reasons she signed up in the first place. I ask questions about classes she would like to take, and goals she would like to accomplish, and at the end I point out that she doesn't seem to want to quit. She agrees, but says she doesn't want to waste the money since she isn't using the facility. I ask if she ever misses appointments, and she says never. Her entire life is dictated by her calendar.

I suggest Personal Training because the appointments will force her to come to the gym, and the trainer can get her started on a routine and a habit. She agrees. We sign the new contract at $29 and personal training for four times a week for three months at a discounted introductory rate. Then we sign her up for a spin class, and she is totally satisfied and smiling. On the way out, she tells the owner to never let me go.

*During that entire encounter, I was actively listening to what she wanted to say. She was angry at herself, not me. I listened to her vent, and then I got her excited about achieving her goals. When we finished the tour, I showed her how to succeed. The personal training appointment was all she needed. She did eventually make her goals, and I can somewhat proudly say that she created the habit of coming to the gym regularly, even without an appointment. **Most of the time your client wants to buy; they were programmed from birth to spend money. All you have to do is actively listen and be a Sales Therapist.***

Notes

Price

v.

Return on Investment

Rookies will always lower the price to get the deal. I call this the "too good to pass up" mentality. For an overwhelming majority of sales, the person selling doesn't comprehend the dollars being spent. Think about it: if you have never run a successful business, you don't understand business finance. Do you think Bill Gates or Warren Buffet stress out about their corporate cell phone expenses? They have a Vice President of Finance and a Corporate Finance Officer. These people have teams that handle the accounts payable, and someone authorizes payment for their monumental seven-figure cell phone bill. If you got that bill, you would think it was a joke. In business, we do not value price. In business, we evaluate the return on investment (ROI). If the business makes more money than it costs to operate, it is successful. So the argument for price is invalid at the business level. But realistically, the price argument should be your last concern for all sales outside of the consumer retail or wholesale environments.

The Practical Application

Five retail stores selling the same make and model of jeans at different prices will train the buyer to be price conscious. It is the sales professional's job to inform the buyer of an ROI sale. Identical cars at two different dealerships with different prices need to be evaluated for ROI. Just because the cars are identical doesn't mean the total price package is identical. What if one dealership wanted $10,000 more for an identical car, but they offered free car washes for life, free maintenance for life, 25 percent off repairs, and when or if you were ever ready for a new car, they would take your trade at retail instead of 20 percent below wholesale? The other dealership is just selling you the car.

Are the two offers identical? Is the extra $10,000 worth the additional services? The trade-in alone would be worth a few thousand dollars, and how much does it cost to get your car washed? What do the oil changes cost over the life of the vehicle? What is the 25-percent discount going to save you over the next 10 years? If you are going to trade the car in next year, it may not be worth the extra money. But if you're going to keep the car for the foreseeable future, it probably is worth the extra ten grand.

The question isn't what can I save you today; it's what can I do to build our long-term relationship? As the dealership offering the extras, I would have great prices on detailing the car. There is, of course, an extra expense, but the detailing cost would be lower than the local detailer's. I would guarantee the return business by taking less profit on the trade-in. During the regular maintenance I would recommend needed services and remind the client of the 25 percent discount. The client paid for these services in advance, and giving the platinum treatment to your clients is the best way to keep them for life. Rookies will always think price first and last.

Notes

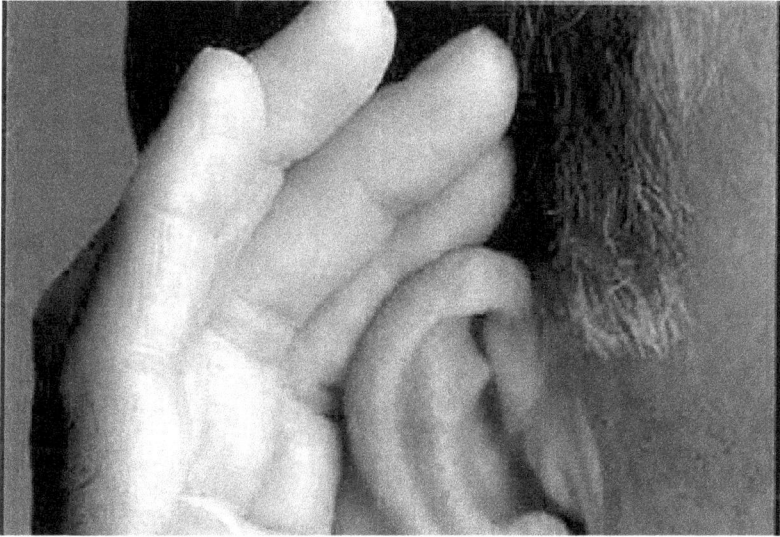

Interrupting Salesperson

One of the first things I teach any sales team is to listen to the client. Consequently, the hardest habit to break for any rookie is "Interrupting Salesperson." Interrupting Salesperson is when the client starts to speak, and you talk over them. You are probably thinking to yourself that interrupting salesperson is a monumentally bad practice, and you are right. However, I guarantee you are guilty of interrupting salesperson every day. Interrupting salesperson is something you have to actively train out of your process. There are several reasons people are guilty of this practice:

1. <u>**The client said something you can directly address with your product.**</u> If the client tells you that their main requirement is something you know your product satisfies, you may just be excited, or you may feel obligated to cut them off to announce your assumed victory.

2. <u>**The client is rambling.**</u> Sometimes clients are trying to think on their feet, and this leads to a broken thought process. You mistake this as confusion or ignorance and assume control of the conversation.

3. <u>**You are an elitist.**</u> You, for some ridiculous reason, have forgotten that the client is the buyer, and you treat them as if they are beneath you. This condescension is probably intrinsically tied to who you are, and you should either correct this severe personality flaw, or find a new career.

4. <u>**You think the client wants you to play a game of fill-in-the-blank.**</u> Every time the client breathes, or takes a moment to organize their thoughts, you jump in to "help" them. This behavior is analogous to finishing words for a person with a stutter. It is rude, annoying, and causes frustration for the client. *Frustrated clients will still buy—just not from you!*

5. **<u>You believe what you have to say is more important than what the client is saying.</u>** I promise: nothing you have to say is more important than what the client is saying.

6. **<u>You are afraid you will forget to highlight some mundane fact if you wait for the client to finish.</u>** This is usually because you are not professional and you don't listen and take notes. If you learn to take notes during client meetings, you can address any client concerns in any order you deem appropriate when the client has finished speaking.

7. **<u>You're a misogynist.</u>** A misogynist is a person who believes women are a lower species, and they treat all women with disdain. The simple solution is to go back to the Stone Age. Women are clients and buyers, and if you want to be a professional salesperson you'll need to treat all clients equally.

8. **<u>You don't realize you are doing it!</u>** This is the most common reason for Interrupting Salesperson. No one ever taught you how to communicate properly, so you were never taught to actively listen to the person with whom you are communicating.

There is a very important distinction between speaking *with* someone versus speaking *at* someone. When you speak *with* someone, you actively listen to your communication partner and reply with thoughtful responses. When you speak *at* someone, neither party is generally listening; both are simply waiting to speak. *Interrupting salespeople are always waiting to speak, and professional salespeople actively listen.*

The most effective sales professionals on the planet understand that 90 percent of their job is counselor/consultant, and 10 percent of their job is facilitator. The number-one priority for a true sales professional is to get the client to talk! Interrupting the client is the same as telling them to shut up; and once you shut the client up, it will be extremely difficult to repair their perception of you, the brand you represent, or your products and services. For these reasons, it is imperative for you to train the interrupting salesperson out of your sales process ASAP, and start actively listening!

What Is Active Listening?

Active Listening is the process of focusing your complete attention on the person speaking. You are actively listening for the following:

• What is being said

• What is *not* being said

• Changes in the tone of the speaker

• When the speaker comes out of their protective shell

• When the speaker shrinks into their protective shell

You are actively looking for the following:

• When the speaker moves to the edge of their seat, or closer to the listener

• When the speaker moves back away from the listener

• When the speaker makes physical contact

• When the speaker crosses legs or arms

• When the speaker turns away from the listener

• When the speaker's eyes are looking left or right

Those are some of the things you are "Actively Listening" for during every conversation. Each one of these things will give you more information so you may communicate accurately.

Current science estimates that only 7 percent of communication is verbal. To put that in perspective, 93 percent of the conversations you have on a daily basis were more than what was said. The easiest way to understand this is by understanding sarcasm. If someone says, "The Cubs are going to win the World Series," but they use a mocking tone, do you believe their assessment, or do you recognize the sarcasm?

The words used were secondary to understanding what was communicated. They were making a joke. If you missed the sarcasm, you became the joke. Your spouse says, "Of course you can go to the strip club! Why would I mind?" But their tone is condescending, not exuberant. Do you go? If you were not actively listening to either of these statements, would you misinterpret the communication? Would you lose face with your friends? Would you lose your spouse?

If you did this with a client, would you lose the business? We actively listen to ensure we understand the communication. *If you are distracted by your own thoughts, you are clearly either waiting to speak or waiting to leave; both options are bad for sales.*

What Does It All Mean?

When you are actively listening, you are *listening* for

- How they are responding to what is being said: you are listening for their needs and wants.

- The questions or topics they are avoiding: you are learning what they are keeping from you.

- The topics that cause a change in their demeanor: you are watching them get excited (wants), attentive (needs), or withdrawn (losing trust).

- The topics they want to discuss further: you are learning what their safe/comfort zone is for your current trust level.

- The topics they lower their voice to discuss: you are learning the gossip, or the taboo truths about the person or business.

When you are "actively listening," you are *looking* for the following:

- When they move to the edge of their seat, or closer to the speaker. This indicates either trust gained or excitement; both are an encouragement to continue.

- When they move back from the speaker. This indicates you are crossing into a trust zone you have *not* earned. Continue with caution by recognizing and explaining your reasoning or thought process to gain the necessary trust.

• When they make physical contact with the speaker. This is a subconscious indication of trust. You don't let people touch you that you don't trust. Some manage ment programs teach the intentional use of this technique to develop trust. If a handshake is considered a neutral social obligation, do you have any other physical contact with the other person? Did they touch your shoulder or your back? Did they say good-bye by shaking with two hands? (The second hand is *not* neutral in the United States, but is a social requirement in most Asian countries.)

• When they cross their legs or arms. This is a subconscious reaction to an uncomfortable situation. Think of this gesture as an imaginary gate; nothing else is getting through while the gate is closed. If someone sits back and crosses their legs "in thought," they are probably thinking of an exit strategy. The best thing you can do is go back to common ground. The one exception to this is during a closing presentation; this action still signifies discomfort, but patience will generally lead to the true objection. (9.9 times out of 10, the objection is their perception of value)

• When they turn away from the speaker. This subconscious action signifies they are preparing to leave. Conversation happens head-on. If the person you are speaking with is subconsciously turning away from you, they are planning a polite exit. If you recognize this action immediately, you can tactically retreat to the last comfort zone and either increase perception of value or improve trust. Pushing forward is a rookie mistake.

• When their eyes are looking left or right during an answer or response. Psychological studies have determined that people subconsciously look to the left when they are remembering something, and they look to the right when they are fabricating something. (Don't believe me? Try to tell your friends a detailed story about the time you met the US president in the Oval Office. They will see you look to your left for mundane facts you have seen on television, and to the right when you discuss the actual meeting and the discussion with the President. Isn't psychology fun?)

The best thing about The Quarter Method is that all of these techniques are dependent upon subconscious responses to perceived stimuli. The client's perceptions of the conversation will elicit very specific involuntary responses. If you are actively listening, and following The Quarter Method training, you will follow these indicators throughout the entire process of the sale, and throughout the development of the relationship.

Notes

NEED v. WANT

I Need a Car.
I Want a Bentley!

Have you as a salesperson ever contemplated why people buy? The core concept is simple: they either *need* something, or they *want* something. The true psychology behind this reality is put into play when you realize that every purchase can have a *want* factor, but not every purchase has a *need* factor. ***Need versus Want is the motivating force behind ALL sales.***

The mindset drives the sale, and as a sales professional, you need to be able to identify "need clients" versus "want clients" as soon as possible. However, as a sales professional, do you know which of the two influential forces is beneficial to you, the salesperson, and the client? The answer is "want." Need-driven buyers are comparison shoppers, and deal searchers, and online buyers. Need-driven sales are generally cold, financially motivated, and thought out. Want-driven buyers, on the other hand, are passionate, and they are in the must-have-this-now mindset. Want-driven buyers buy brands, and accessories, and "bells and whistles."

Your job, as the salesperson, is to turn need-driven buyers into want-driven buyers. The number-one reason there is a sales profession is to satisfy that one main requirement. The salesperson is expected by their employer to be able to use skill and guile to convert need buyers into want buyers. If the buyer comes to buy a minivan, the salesperson's job is to affect the buyer's psychology enough to change the buyer from "a minivan" to "This Minivan." Your competitor sells "a minivan," but only you have "This Minivan."

Sales professionals get the buyer excited! We sell the *want*. Want comes at a higher price, and *a true sales professional will get you so excited to own the product or service that the price becomes secondary, tertiary, or even irrelevant.* Because a sales professional is actively listening before the handshake, the excitement and perception of value created by the professional during the sales process will practically guarantee elite closing percentages.

You may have heard or used the term "Hot Buttons." This is used to associate the client's wants and needs. A buyer purchasing their first minivan by trading in their sports car might be interested in a minivan with an upgraded sport suspension package and an increased horsepower option. These bonuses come at a higher cost, but if it is what the client wants, it's the sales professional's job to satisfy the buyer before they leave. If the salesperson didn't pay attention to the buyer and just let them test a standard minivan, the buyer may not be satisfied, and they will go to a competitor. The point is, if the salesperson is actively listening and is asking the right questions, the client's "Hot Buttons" will be obvious. Satisfy all of the "Hot Buttons," and you will more than satisfy the client. Let me explain this advanced concept with an example that allows for easy comprehension.

To get from the start of a race to the finish line, you need a vehicle. If the only requirement is completion, any vehicle will do. What vehicle do you get for the "race"? Anything with an engine and wheels will work; technically, I could use a riding mower. But some people choose very specific cars. The Need is simply to finish the race. But the Want is to finish _____.

Whatever you filled in the blank with just identified *your* wants. The salesperson's job is to get this information from the buyer. The best way to accomplish this goal is to ask questions. Fill-in-the-blank questions tend to be the most effective method because they focus the conversation. Remember, it is imperative for the client/buyer to communicate their needs and wants. Let them speak! Use the fill-in-the-blank technique after identifying the needs, and once the client has given an idea of their wants. The fill-in-the-blank question defines details and provides truth. Here are some examples:

1. When I drive my new minivan, I want the ride to be _____.

2. When people see me in my new minivan, I want them to notice _____.

3. If someone challenges me to a race, I will

   _____.

4. When I am on the freeway and I use the accelerator, I want the van to _____.

These are just examples of fill-in-the-blank questions to use on the buyer. What if the buyer said they wanted a base-model minivan, but all of the answers to the above questions would only be satisfied by the top-of-the-line minivan? Which one should the salesperson have them test-drive first? The answer is, whichever they wanted to drive first. I would simply explain the truth of their reality and let them decide. Don't let your ego or your arrogance cost you a deal or hurt the brand you represent. *Help the client make a decision. Do not force, or strong-arm, or intimidate, or lie.* Selling the base model is better than not selling anything. *If you are trying to convince the client, you have already stopped listening; you are simply waiting to speak.*

Notes

The Art of Sales!

I have heard sales described as an art form, but this is not the whole truth. Sales is a scientific and psychological process that follows a prescribed course to achieve a desired outcome. Being a salesperson is a skilled professional career, like being a lawyer or a doctor. Instead of medical school or law school, the sales professional goes to the school of hard knocks. Sales professionals learn through a tested system of on-the-job training and failure. The longer you are successful at sales, the more successful you will be at sales. I know that sounds like circular logic, but it is a concrete truth.

The reason for this truth is psychology. People who have been selling for years have learned from countless mistakes. They have developed the ability to "read" new clients, and they have learned to value themselves and their services. When all of these confidence-builders amalgamate with wisdom, experience, and product mastery, the end result becomes the artist.

One of the best compliments I can receive from a client is, "This was so easy! I really had no intention of buying anything today, but you made the experience so simple and empowering, how could I say no?"

Yes, I do have clients say that, or something like that, on a regular basis. Sales is only an art form when the client doesn't feel like they are being sold. *If the client becomes frustrated, angry, belligerent, or withdrawn, you are* **not** *an artist; you are a bully!* Sales is easy...if you have a well-developed system, a professional training program, and professionally developed sales and incentives. However, sales is combat when you have none of these. If you look at potentials as marks to be taken advantage of instead of long-term clients with needs and wants for you to satisfy, you are a con artist; please stop calling what you do "sales."

How I Met My Wife

Everyday in sales is a mystery. Even though I am probably selling the same product, the client is always different. Yes, even reorder clients are different. Are you exactly the same every day, or do you have good days and bad days, great days, and days you should have stayed in bed? The beauty of being a true sales professional is that every opportunity to sell is fresh. I need to start my process from hello and continue through to the close, and I need to do this without the client feeling like it's robotic.

On one particular day back in 2003 I was managing a fitness facility when one of the members comes in with a guest pass for her friend five minutes before the class they wanted to take. Now, contrary to popular belief, fitness centers are not altruistic places that love to give away free things. Guest passes are a tool for you to be able to bring your friends in so we can sign them up and get you a workout buddy. In essence, the member and the salesperson are on the same team, and their

81

ulterior motive is to get the friend to sign up. This reality was reinforced whenever a member asked for guest passes. It goes without saying that the opportunity to sell happens prior to the workout or the class to be taken. The reason for this is simple: I can't force you to stay after class for a sales process, and honestly, neither of us wants you exhausted and dripping with sweat during the sales presentation.

So on this particular day, I told the member to enjoy her class, but her friend and I were going to sit down and get to know each other and discuss her current workout routine, her fitness goals, and her life story. I then rushed the member off as she complained about the process, and introduced myself to her guest. The first words she said to me were, "I'm not buying anything!" Not "hello," "how are you," "I didn't catch your name," or "we almost got away with it." She started our conversation with "I'm not buying anything!"

Some of you may be thinking this was aggressive and confrontational, and you would be right. For you active listeners, her arms were crossed, her legs were crossed, and her body was facing away from me. She had just drawn a line in the sand. But I rolled with it and told her that was fine and that she didn't have to buy anything. I then told her the tour and presentation were formalities before I could activate her seven-day pass. Instantly she relaxed her aggressive posture, and I explained the process for the tour and the presentation.

"First we sit here and get to know each other. Then I will take you on a tour of the facility, and finally we will discuss the membership you are not going to buy, and after that you can join your friend."

She smiles at my little sarcastic poke and agrees. I start with the bread and butter: open-ended questions. What is your current daily routine? How often do you work out? Where else do you exercise? And so on. by the end of the getting-to-know you phase of the sales process, I have already discovered that she enjoys working out, but that she will not come in without an appointment or an extremely reliable workout partner. She is *excited about the Group Ex classes, and she would like to be stronger.*

We start the tour, and I can see her getting more excited as she sees more of the facility. Her speech changes from "the classes" to "my classes," and she starts owning the membership on the tour by saying things like "I would be here three to four times a week." At the end of the tour, we sit down to discuss the membership, and I can see her body language has completely changed. She is facing me and listening intently. Her legs and arms are no longer crossed, and she is smiling and laughing. I go over the rates for membership and explain that the only way for her to be successful is if she commits to the lifestyle change, and the only way she will do that is if she starts with a personal trainer for the first three months at three times a week. She agrees, and we fill out the paperwork. I introduce her to her trainer, we set her first three appointments, and $3,500 later she is leaving with a new membership and personal training.

All of this started with the words, "I'm not buying anything!" To me, that's like smacking a lion on the nose with a steak and saying, "You can't catch me." Game on! At this point, my wife always points out that we started dating a few months later, and that I eventually paid off those credit cards. Game, set, and match to the wife.

Notes

Peer Pressure, Social Psychology, and Sales

Just as there are various industries in sales, there are various disciplines in psychology. In Social Psychology we study social behavior and how it is influenced by society. Specifically, for sales, we are interested in two very distinct social traits: Normative Influence and Effective Frequency.

Normative Influence

Normative influence is directly related to societal influence leading to conformity. You're probably more familiar with the term "peer pressure." Technically, it is defined as the influence of other people that leads us to be liked or accepted by them. Normative influence will force public compliance even if there is no private acceptance. Or, put simply, there are no zebras in a herd of antelope.

Think of it this way: You just started a new job on an open sales floor. Everyone in the company drinks Starbucks coffee, but you prefer donut-shop coffee. Every day someone makes a comment about your coffee. How long before you start putting your coffee in a Starbucks cup, or until you switch to Starbucks?

Let's say you refuse to do either; you refuse to conform. Would you be surprised six weeks into your new job if you were let go? The reason given was that you just never really fit in with the rest of the company. I know it sounds ridiculous, but people are driven by their subconscious psychology. Groups form for security and anonymity; by not conforming, you are the zebra in the herd of antelope.

This simple psychological truth is prevalent in everything you do in society. As we have previously discussed, only 7 percent of communication is verbal. By not conforming, the remaining 93 percent of your communication was, "I am not part of this group." Bearing that in mind, the group was obligated to leave you behind because you wouldn't conform. You reveled in your black-and-white striped splendor, but the group saw you as a risk they couldn't allow. Goodbye, zebra! Society often hinges on these subtle, yet generally imperceptible moments.

You are probably wondering how this affects sales. Well, the affect of the normative influence on sales is both monumental and, again, generally imperceptible. This is the deeper reason behind the want, and the most common answer to why. Why does the buyer want a high-performance minivan? What societal influence is causing his behavioral change from a sports car to a performance minivan? You must understand that these influences exist, and they are constantly affecting the world around you. You need to recognize when the zebra is conforming to become an antelope, and if you want to truly satisfy the buyer, you need to find out why.

Effective Frequency

One of the ways a sales professional can affect the Normative Influence is by first understanding, and then applying, Effective Frequency. Effective Frequency is the number of times a person must be exposed to a brand or product before they are psychologically driven to conform.

Thomas Smith wrote a guide called *Successful Advertising* in 1885. The analogy he used is still in use today:

• The first time people look at any given ad, they don't even see it.

• The second time, they don't notice it.

• The third time, they are aware that it is there.

- The fourth time, they have a fleeting sense that they've seen it somewhere before.

- The fifth time, they actually read the ad.

- The sixth time they thumb their nose at it.

- The seventh time, they start to get a little irritated with it.

- The eighth time, they start to think, "Here's that confounded ad again."

- The ninth time, they start to wonder if they're missing out on something.

- The tenth time, they ask their friends and neighbors if they've tried it.

- The eleventh time, they wonder how the company is paying for all these ads.

- The twelfth time, they start to think that it must be a good product.

- The thirteenth time, they start to feel the product has value.

- The fourteenth time, they start to remember wanting a product exactly like this for a long time.

- The fifteenth time, they start to yearn for it because they can't afford to buy it.

- The sixteenth time, they accept the fact that they will buy it sometime in the future.

- The seventeenth time, they make a note to buy the product.

- The eighteenth time, they curse their poverty for not allowing them to buy this terrific product.

- The nineteenth time, they count their money very carefully.

- *The twentieth time prospects see the ad, they buy!*

If you brand and advertise your product consistently and effectively, people are psychologically driven to buy the product so they will be liked and accepted by other people. This starts a chain reaction called the Normative Influence.

Obviously there are no concrete numbers for Effective Frequency. Since everyone is affected by their own psychology differently, we can only theorize about the number of exposures needed. What we do know is that there is no such thing as too much advertising. Brand everything, and advertise that brand everywhere. *The amount of times people see your branded product is directly related to the number of people buying your product.* As the wave of popularity builds, so will your sales. The fun way of looking at this conundrum is, "As more people buy it, more people will want to buy it!"

Notes

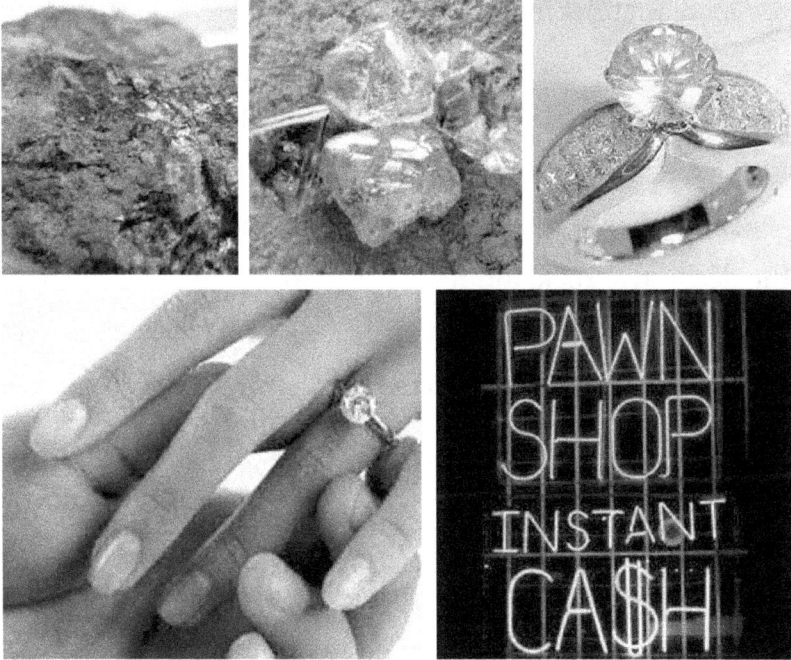

Perceived Value

What is value?

Value is defined as (NOUN) *The regard that something is held to deserve; the importance, worth, or usefulness of something.* (VERB) *To estimate the money worth of something.*

Idealogically, value is simply a perception. For example, think of a wedding ring. A wedding ring is a piece of pretty metal that is sometimes decorated with pretty rocks. If I own the mine that the metal came from, what are a few grams of metal worth? If I own the mine with the decorative rocks, what are the rocks worth? The jeweler who turns the metal into a ring will obviously add to the value of the metal, generally based on market perception. The jeweler that cuts the decorative rock and makes it sparkle will definitely add to the value of the decorative rock, and that jeweler's end product is graded on a scale to determine the value. The jeweler that combines the metal and the decorative rock will again increase the value.

Finally, once the ring is placed on a finger during a ceremony, the value will skyrocket for the current owner. But, as an epilogue to this story, what if the happily-ever-after wasn't as pretty or as durable as the ring? How much is the once priceless ring worth on the secondary market? The answer to all of these questions is exactly the same: ***The value is whatever the buyer perceives the product (in this case, a wedding ring) to be worth.*** The seller ***always*** starts at a disadvantage. ***It is the seller's job to increase the perception of value.*** To do that, the seller must gather information about the buyer. The seller must ask questions. If you constantly find yourself in a price war, you are *not* increasing the perceived value of "your" product. You are not special!

Perceived Value & Urgency

The "perceived value" of any product and its "urgency" are established by the person selling! For a majority of sales, the buyer does not necessarily need the product, and even if they do need a product, there is generally no urgency to purchase the product right now. This is a psychological control mechanism created to control the normative-influence response. For our purposes, we'll call this the "let me think about it" safety switch. This safety switch is developed over time and after numerous experiences with "bottom-feeder" aggressive salespeople. It is a programmed response to any and all sales situations.

This safety switch prevents the would-be buyer from blowing the rent money on every shiny trinket they see. This can be very frustrating to a "bottom feeder" salesperson, but for a sales professional, it is simply an expected psychological response, and it can usually be addressed by the deliberate incremental increases in value throughout the sales process. The professional salesperson understands the value of "Want," and they always guide the client from feigned interest to *need* and then to *want*. If your sales process is missing these important psychological milestones, you are a "bottom feeder."

Value Exercise

Widget Salesperson 1 sells based on quantity and cost. The sales presentation is limited to numbers, and profit per item is limited.

Salesperson: Mr. Jones, I can get you 10,000 widgets for 10 cents each.

Mr. Jones: Why would I want 10,000 widgets?

Salesperson: They make excellent giveaways for your clients/customers.

Mr. Jones: Are they branded?

Salesperson: Yes! Every one of the widgets has our company branding and our phone number.

Mr. Jones: Why would I want to distribute your branded material? Can you put my company's branding and phone number on them?

Salesperson: No. I'm afraid that isn't even an option.

Mr. Jones: In that case, I'll take the 10,000, but at 4 cents each.

Salesperson: I can only go as low as 5 cents.

Mr. Jones: Okay.

This deal was sold for $500, but the widget profit started at 4 cents. The company selling the widget only made $100 on the deal. What do you think they made after overhead? What do you think the commission was worth?

However:

Widget Salesperson 2 sells on relationship, value, needs, and wants. The sales presentation includes color options, branding options, direct-shipping options, and lots of charm and personality. The profit per item is massive, and the client feels a connection to the company.

Sales Professional: Yes, Mr. Jones, I can get you 10,000 widgets.

Mr. Jones: Great! As we discussed, this will be a great value-add for our clients/customers.

Sales Professional: Of course, for a little more, we can have them made with your company colors.

Mr. Jones: That would be great!

Sales Professional: I can also have your branding printed on each piece at an extremely reasonable price.

Mr. Jones: How much will these benefits increase the cost?

Sales Professional: The better question is, which division's budget can best absorb the expense?

Mr. Jones: What do you mean?

Sales Professional: Once we have the widget manufactured in your company colors, with your company brand and your phone number or website, this expense should go against your marketing budget. Generally, the marketing division has a bigger budget, and marketing expenses are not expected to turn an immediate profit.

Mr. Jones: I hadn't considered that. But I still have to justify the expense, so what will these widgets cost?

Sales Professional: What would you expect to pay for a high-quality, branded, marketing piece?

Mr. Jones: I won't pay more than $1.25 each.

Sales Professional: So if I can get the price below $1.25, are you ready to sign today?

Mr. Jones: I think I could be. How far below $1.25 are we talking?

Sales Professional: Before I can answer that, I have one more question regarding your needs.

Mr. Jones: Shoot.

Sales Professional: Do you have the warehouse space to store 10,000 of these widgets, or would you prefer we warehoused the widgets and sent them wherever you need them, at minimal shipping cost?

Mr. Jones: You can do that?

Sales Professional: Of course. And when you start to run low, I'll call you and see if you want to do a reorder, or if you would like to discuss a different product.

Mr. Jones: If I want to do a reorder, is my rate guaranteed?

Sales Professional: Within a reasonable margin increase, yes. However, if something happens to drive the widget price too high, I would of course meet with you to arrange other options.

Mr. Jones: So you would become my go-to guy for these marketing items?

Sales Professional: And any other product I have access to supplying.

Mr. Jones: Well then, let's draw this up.

Sales Professional: My pleasure, Mr. Jones.

This deal was sold for $12,500. With all of the marketing benefits added, the widget profit started at 20 cents per piece. The company selling the widget made $10,500 on the deal. What do you think they made after overhead? What do you think the commission was worth?

Did the Sales Professional push the price, or satisfy the client's needs and wants? Cost per item becomes secondary with a "perceived" increase in value. People buy based on perceived value!

Five factors affect perceived value:

1. Sell on quality
2. Sell on need
3. Sell on want
4. Sell on desire
5. **Never sell on cost!**

Start asking open-ended questions to find "hot buttons." Use these "hot buttons" to target interests in quality, needs, wants, and desires.

(You probably noticed the use of want *and* desire *as two different things. Although the two words are synonymous, they are not identical.* Desire *is a much stronger psychological response to passion. When you want something, you are identifying a stronger attachment than a need. When you desire something, you are identifying a stronger attachment than a basic want. When you desire something, it becomes a passion.*

Desire is usually associated with something you must have at all costs. I may want a Ferrari, but if I can't afford to buy a Ferrari, I will accept this reality and move on with my life. However, if I desire a Ferrari, I will sacrifice everything to own one. I would change my lifestyle and my values to be able to acquire a Ferrari. If the desire is strong enough, I may steal a Ferrari.

Desire is a degree of emotion that identifies what you are willing to do to achieve a result. Your goal as a Sales Professional is to increase the perception of value to such a degree that the client desires your product. People in this mindset do not *argue price!)*

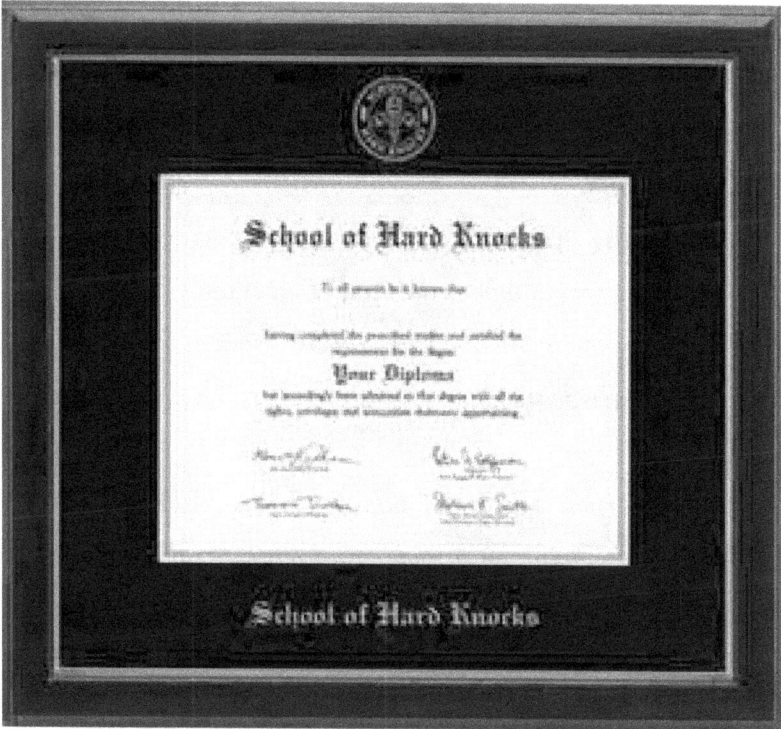

"Learning to Tie Your Shoes"

Throughout my career, I have had the privilege of training and managing numerous sales teams. Based on my experience, I can tell you with 100 percent certainty that no matter how great your sales process, your team will always try to change the system. Please understand: I am a huge proponent of constantly evaluating your system for improvements, and making changes when necessary. That is not what I am referring to in this situation. What I am referring to is your sales team becoming cocky, lazy, or complacent.

The true test for any sales system is rookie success ratios. If I bring on a rookie and teach them the sales process and they are successful for the first few months but then the numbers fall off, the cause is the natural human instinct toward complacency. The system worked, but then, after tasting success, the salesperson starts to skip steps. They become egotistical and start to believe they are the success factor. They change the sales process because they are, all of a sudden, too good to follow the system that made them money. The well dries up, and so do the paychecks. The only thing left is the ego. Then it's someone else's fault, and they fail, and instead of starting over, they become yet another statistic.

The important thing to remember in this situation is proactive is way better than reactive. Update your process to correct this problem before it becomes a problem. During your morning meetings, remind your team of the evils of complacency, and then remind them of the money they get from following the process step by step, obsessively. I have seen this happen thousands of times, and I promise your team will not recognize what they are doing until they are broke and broken.

I remember one team of above-average salespeople whom I had trained to follow my sales system. They were killing the sales! Above-average closing ratios, amazing pipelines, great attitudes, and it was raining money. Then, literally, from one month to the next, it all died. Instinctively knowing the problem, I called the team into a meeting to discuss process. I went around the room asking about our sales process, and made them admit that they had all become too egotistical and complacent.

Then I made them learn by association. I told them all to bring in lace-up shoes. They went to their cars and came back looking bewildered. Then I told them to untie their shoes; they did so. I told them they had 20 minutes to retie their shoes, but they could not use any familiar shoe-tying system. In the next 20 minutes they had to create a new way to tie their shoes, and then be able to show everyone their new process. I then left the room and came back 20 minutes later to a room full of untied shoes.

My entire sales team looked angry, frustrated, and beaten. The exercise seemed simple enough, but the practical application proved to be way more complex. I asked some open-ended questions like, "Why aren't your shoes tied?" or "What seems to be the problem?" I received feedback on some of their attempts and what caused the failure. Then, finally, I asked why they would try to reinvent my sales process if they couldn't create a new process for something as simple as tying their shoes.

The light bulbs started going off, and we used the rest of the hour to refresh their memories regarding the established sales process. One by one, we went around the room and everyone has an epiphany about their little ego excursion into brokesville. Then we agreed to watch out for this obviously stupid mistake in the future.

The new team competitions became: qualified prospects, prospects moved forward in the sales process, and referrals closed. The team went right back to killing the sales, and all of a sudden it was raining money again.

The point is this: even the best get lazy. Your system should compensate for these little hiccups before they become profit killers. The sales manager should be less like a jockey at the Kentucky Derby and more like a cowboy on a cattle drive. It is the sales manager's job to guide the team home and to correct for wandering calves. If you lose too many calves on the cattle drive, maybe you're not the best cowboy for the job.

Notes

4 out of 5
Dentists
From a Tiny Office in the Suburbs
Agree!

The Numbers

Ninety-seven percent of all statistics are made up! (Including this one!) Statistics are a sales and marketing tool! Some are legitimate; most are made up! Legitimate statistics are based on the results from a limited research group, and are therefore an educated guess at best. Statistics are effective because people are herd animals, and herd animals like to follow the rest of the herd. This simple fact is why there is a Normative Influence behavior correction.

To be a part of the herd, you *must* fit in with the herd. Remember, there are no zebras in a herd of antelope.

Therefore, marketing and advertising professionals invent statistics they can "validate" in an effort to make you comply with the normative influence. If they are introducing a new product, they associate the product with positive emotions or experiences and say things like, "Four out of five dentists agree," or "your neighbors shop here too!"

All marketing and advertising statistics are designed to make you think that a majority of the herd approves of your decision to buy, thereby making it okay for you to buy the product. This is an extremely effective technique for manipulating the herd, and it should be used as often as feasibly possible. Your job is to sell the product, preferably to people who want the product. This technique doesn't make people buy something they don't want; it helps them to buy something they *do* want, but they might need a subconscious psychological approval to feel right about the decision.

When you are inventing a statistic, you will use a number above 60 percent (majority of the herd) for stats in your favor, and a number below 40 percent (minority of the herd) for stats against your current objection. The 20 points between 40 and 60 percent are considered neutral, and generally will not create psychological sway.

Like it or not, this is the reality of sales, or how to manipulate the herd. You control the herd by manipulating a few animals in the front! The rest of the herd just follows the animal in front of them (i.e., celebrity endorsements).

Important point: Don't lie about your product with statistics. You will be called out. Created statistics should be something the client can't argue, such as

• "About 80 percent of my clients buy that product."

• "I have a 100-percent satisfaction rating from clients who bought that product."

• "My last five clients were excited that I even had these in stock."

These statements will subconsciously satisfy the normative influence requirement. After that, the trick is to make sure you are using hot buttons to get the client the product they wanted! Never speak negatively about a competitor. It's unprofessional, and it can destroy the trust you have built with the client. Instead, highlight similarities and strengths, such as

- "Yes, of course we offer spa services, and there is no additional cost for the towel service."

- "We offer the same unlimited-everything plan, but we include free hotspot service as well."

- "Yes, I have numerous Corvettes on the property, and they all come with lifetime free maintenance."

These statements tell the client that they are in the right place. With one sentence, you have begun to increase the perception of value. When you have mastered your sales process, you will be able to raise the client's perception of value consistently throughout the consultation, and you will increase your percentages.

Selling to the "Alpha"

As we have already discussed, humans are pack/herd animals. The distinction between pack and herd is psychological. People who take risks, build businesses or companies that are responsible for employees, and several other pack leader traits, are in a pack. Everyone else is in a herd. A CEO that came up the ranks is in a herd. A CEO that started with nothing but a dream is in a pack.

For ease of understanding we will use the sheep analogy for herd people, and the wolf analogy for the pack people. Most major corporations are headed by sheep. This is not an insult. Sheep are an integral part of the business model. Sheep turn the wheel. The fundamental difference is risk. Wolves accept risk as part of their nature. Sheep start at the bottom of their respective fields and slowly work their way to the top. Wolves understand that they may starve or they may succeed, but the result will be entirely their doing. Sheep need the security blanket of the time clock and the steady paycheck. Sheep work for someone; wolves create.

The reason the distinction is important is because there are a lot of sheep that think they are alphas, but they are just the lead sheep in the herd. Because of this fact, they are easily manipulated by a true wolf. All Sales Professionals are Wolves. Bad salespeople and bottom-feeder salespeople are simply deluded sheep. If you follow your sales process, you will control the sale and the outcome.

<u>Lead Sheep v. Herd Sheep</u>

The only difference between a lead sheep and a herd sheep is the way they are manipulated! A lead sheep likes to be in charge. The sales professional will recognize this weakness and use it to gain an advantage. The simple process to use on a lead sheep is to give them the decision authority over a limited set of choices. The lead sheep thinks they are in charge because they are making the decisions, but the sales professional is the one who gave them the limited options, and is therefore in control of the sale. This is still the wolf leading the sheep, but the sheep thinks they are in charge.

117

Notes

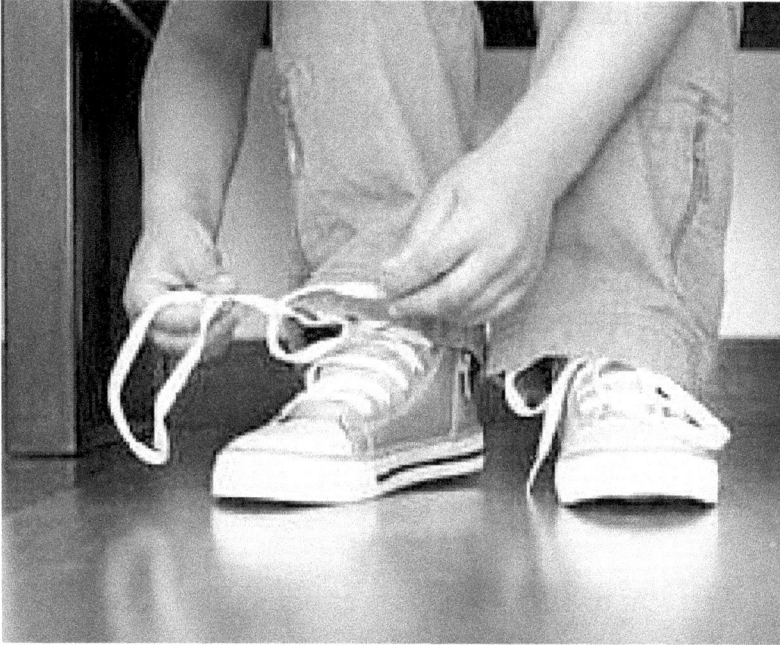

What Defines Success?

As we have already discussed, *all* statistics are made up. Bearing that in mind, here are some sales statistics you can readily find on the Internet. The source doesn't matter, since they're made up or best guess! These statistics, like all statistics, are intended to help you learn by association with personal experience. When you see a statistic, the first thing you should do is determine what is being sold. The second thing you should do is determine who is selling the product or idea. Finally, you should evaluate the validity of the claim (i.e., "Four out of five dentists in a small office in the suburbs and own stock in the gum company" is not the same as "four out of five dentists globally").

Using this technique, consider these statistics to help you with your sales.

• 47 percent of salespeople stop after the first no.
  (That's almost half of your competition—gone!)

• 68 percent of salespeople stop after the second no.

• 82 percent of salespeople stop after the third no.

• 94 percent of salespeople stop after the fourth no.

• 6 percent of salespeople will ask for the fifth close.

How do your own numbers compare with these statistics? How do your coworkers' numbers compare?

How the Market Psychology Works

Studies have indicated that over 60 percent of consumers say "no" four times before they are comfortable enough to make a purchase. Let that sink in for a minute. Even if they wanted to buy the product, 60 percent of your clients are psychologically driven to say "*no*" four times before they are comfortable with the purchase.

Combine that little nugget of gold with the statistic that only 6 percent of salespeople will consistently ask for the fifth close, and it's a wonder anything gets sold. Or is it? Forty percent of your clients are still unaccounted for. If 20–25 percent of those clients are price buyers, that leaves us with 15–20 percent of your clients as unidentified. Now we factor in the "average" closing percentage of 10–20 percent. The overwhelming disparity between sales professionals and rookies is approximately 1 out of 100. Therefore, it is extremely plausible that 60 percent of your business deals are being closed only 6 percent of the time.

If that statistic is accurate enough to be validated, that means to control over 60 percent of the market opportunities, you need to close more than four times. Make sure, however, to get a "yes" on several trial closes before you ask for a solid money close. Trial closes are questions you ask to keep the buyer involved in the process. Objectively, a trial close is used every time the perception of value needs to increase. Subjectively, using trial closes as an integral part of your sales process eliminates complications during the money close, and makes the closing portion of your sales process a formality. I will discuss the sales process in further detail in *The Quarter Method, Book 2: Communicating in High Definition* and in *The Quarter Method, Book 3: Closing Linguistics.*

GOING OUT OF BUSINESS!
EVERYTHING MUST GO!

When Is It Okay
to Lower the Price?

When is it okay to lower your price? The answer is, when the price correction is justified by something more than your fear of losing the deal. Think about what you're asking. Did the product/service become less valuable after you presented the cost? Unless you are price gouging your clients, you really can't afford to lower the price. If you are gouging your clients, stop it; that kind of predatory sales process will eventually destroy your brand. In today's digital reality, the client walks into the deal with an idea of the price range for most purchases.

If you are more expensive without justification, you are probably losing a lot of deals for that reason alone. If you think the one client out of ten is worth the risk, you are still living in the 1960s and you need to be introduced to the power of social media.

Consider your true cost of overhead. How much do you need to include in each deal to be profitable? If you are adding in more than 20–30 percent for profit, you are gouging. If your salespeople are increasing the cost for a larger commission, they are hurting your brand. That's one of the reasons you have a Sales Manager.

Your Sales Manager is responsible for two fundamental realities. The first and foremost responsibility of the Sales Manager is sales-revenue generation. The second responsibility is to protect the brand from internal harm. Every Loss Prevention Specialist will tell you that the biggest theft category is generally employees, just as I will tell you that the biggest threats to your brand are all internal. A corrupt or inept sales force can destroy your brand in a few months. Additionally, bad business practices will destroy your brand just as quickly.

Once you have all of your true costs, you can add in profit per item and therefore profit per deal. As we have already discussed, perception of value is the only reality when it comes to pricing your product or service. Some elite brands have significant markups associated with their brands.

For example, there is no such thing as a pair of $500 denim jeans. However, if the brand has developed a perception of value that is high enough for people to pay $500 for a pair of jeans, the owners of the brand are doing exactly what you should be doing. If the rest of the market is in a specific and accepted price range, and you are selling at a 2,000 percent increase to unsuspecting buyers, you are price gouging. There is a difference between a highly valued product and opportunist pricing. I concede that the difference is primarily ethical, but unethical businesses don't usually succeed at the lower levels of business.

Bearing all of these factors in mind, how much can you afford to take out of any deal?

Clients usually ask for a price decrease for a few reasons:

1. You didn't raise the perception of value high enough for the decision maker.

2. It can't hurt to ask!

3. Experience has taught them that the request is usually rewarded by a nervous salesperson.

4. They want a discount to compete against another bid.

5. And in a few cases, they simply can't afford it.

I always default to the lack of perception of value first, and here's why. In the fairy tale "Jack and the Beanstalk," Jack is given all the money the family has to go and buy food so the family won't starve. The "bean salesman" does such a great job of increasing the perception of value that Jack buys the beans even though his family may starve. Jack didn't go home to ask his mother, or negotiate price; he bought the beans and ran home excited.

I realize this is a fairy tale, but it does teach us a lot about human nature and morals. Humans want to believe in you and your product. Deep down in the core of their being, they want to believe in you, and thereby in human nature. The salesman in the fairy tale is represented as a con man, but the truth is always more complex. Remember, sales is a job or a career; people do sales to earn a living or to feed their family. When you lower your price, you are lowering your profit. If lowering your price is part of your system, then you will put yourself out of business. Your salespeople will lose their jobs and they won't be able to feed their families. If supply and demand is the first law of business economics, then cause and effect is the first law of the universe.

Maintain pricing standards by creating a sales system that increases perception of value incrementally from start to finish. **If occasionally you must lower the price to close the deal, you must negotiate something in return.** That may be something as simple as a signed deal right now, or as complex as a three-consecutive-order guarantee. To maintain the equality of both parties, both parties must concede something. If you give the discount with no concessions from the client, you are putting the client in a position of control, and that will inevitably spiral out of control until you lose the deal, the client, and all future business and referrals. Sales Professionals nod approval at this truth, while rookies, aggressive sales predators, and deluded sheep verbally disagree with it.

Notes

The Wolf v. Sheep Analogy

I have used the Wolf v. Sheep analogy to define the psychological differences between sales professionals and clients because this is the closest natural association for several reasons:

- There are a lot more sheep than there are wolves.

- Sheep and clients gather in large groups and are easily spooked by their peers.

- Wolves work alone or in small groups and are extremely competitive with outside packs.

- When a sheep wakes up in the morning, it eats the food provided.

- When a wolf wakes up in the morning, he must find the sheep.

- The sheep usually have several layers of protection specifically designed to keep the wolf out.

- The grass/paycheck for a sheep is readily available; the sheep simply goes to where the grass grows.

- Wolves must first find the sheep, then outsmart the sheep, and then finish the hunt to eat just one meal. This process is the daily routine for all true wolves.

• Aside from the daily struggle to eat, the wolf must also contend with other wolves trying to catch the same sheep.

As I have already identified, unsuccessful or dishonest salespeople are just deluded sheep! These are people with no cunning, no artistry, and no skill. They are the ones you are probably competing against for the deal, and their favorite close is the improperly used sharp-angle close, or what I call the price-drop close.

The price-drop close is an act of desperation and an obvious sign of a deluded sheep. Price is rarely the true objection, but with no cunning or skill, the deluded sheep is always desperate for the sale. Deluded sheep never focus on the client's needs/wants, and with none of the client's vital information available, the deluded sheep will lose the deal.

Upon recognizing this truth, the deluded sheep will try to make the deal too good to pass by lowering their price. This inexplicable price reduction will kill the deluded sheep's profit margin and begin a price war with any other deluded sheep in the process.

A true wolf will ask open-ended questions to gain more knowledge; and with this information, they will maintain price. While the deluded sheep are competing to see who is willing to lose more on the deal, the true wolf will gain the client's trust, develop perception of value, and close on quality or benefits. Wolves know there are millions of sheep in the herd, and that the sheep want to be led. Closing the deal simply requires the wolf to maintain control, and outsmart the sheep!

Likeability Equals Success!

If people genuinely like you, they will want to buy from you. Conversely, if people think you are an arrogant S.O.B. or an elitist, they will want you out of their lives. More importantly, for the Sales Professional, they will *not* buy from you!

A true wolf, or Sales Professional, understands this basic rule of psychology and makes it a priority to find common ground with the client. A Sales Professional actively listens to the client and provides the best possible solution. A deluded sheep genuinely believes they are better than the client, and treats all clients with disdain. I have met so many really smart people who thought they were "too good to do sales" or thought selling the product was beneath them. In all cases, they failed.

Sales is always a competition! Someone always wins, and someone always loses! You should prepare for all sales appointments by deciding to win, and then set an action plan to make it happen. Your sales process should be ingrained into who you are, and how you sell. If you "just wing it" with every client, you are a deluded sheep. I will discuss the sales process in further detail in *The Quarter Method, Book 2: Communicating in High Definition* and in *The Quarter Method, Book 3: Closing Linguistics*.

Fail to Plan, Plan to Fail!

Every sale is familiar, and every sale is completely different. A Sales Professional approaches every potential client with one truth: the only thing you know walking in the door is your product. You need to gather all pertinent information from the potential client to close the deal. You may be selling the same product to two companies in the same industry, but because you are dealing with different people, you should prepare as if they are completely different. Yes, you should know all of the relevant industry-specific information, but you do *not* know how the client wants to apply the product to their company.

If during the course of the sales process it becomes apparent that the client trusts your expertise, you must handle the opportunity like a professional and earn the trust you have already been given. Some clients are going to be less informed, while others may be incompetent business owners, and still others know every aspect of their business. The only way for you to determine which client you are dealing with is by asking open-ended questions and actively listening to the client. If they like you, they will like the company and product you represent! I will discuss the sales process in further detail in *The Quarter Method, Book 2: Communicating in High Definition* and in *The Quarter Method, Book 3: Closing Linguistics.*

Wrapping It All Up

Don't be stopped by the first rejection! Remember, psychologically, humans don't feel comfortable with a purchase until they have said "no" four times. You could use this to your advantage by simply changing your perspective from "no means no!" to "no the first four times means 'not yet.'" Another way of looking at this statistically is, "no the first *four* times just means, 'You haven't sold me yet!'"

Success is not a mystery. Your clients "wouldn't have gotten away with it if it weren't for you meddlin' salespeople." Sales Professionals are not successful because they want to be. They are successful because they plan to be, and they plan for all possible outcomes leading to the close. Bad salespeople, rookies, or deluded sheep, hope and pray for luck, and then they price drop in desperation when that doesn't work. Which were you yesterday? Which will you be tomorrow?

The Quarter Method Sales Training System is a process that will take time to master. If you apply these techniques to your sales system, you will become more successful. Remember, the average human needs to successfully practice 1,000 times to achieve mastery. That's 1,000 successes to become a master. The number of failures you add to the total will depend on several factors:

1. Consistency: Don't fall back into your old habits.

2. Follow through: Before, during and after every deal, you should be evaluating each stage of your system for successes and failures. Once you discover a recurring weakness, it can be corrected.

3. Willingness to change: I have personally known numerous people with below-10-percent closing averages who thought they were amazing at sales. In their opinion, the problem was always the client. *Remember, it is not the client's job to buy; it is your job to sell!*

4. Are you Actively Listening, or waiting to speak?

5. Did you incrementally increase the perception of value from start to finish?

6. Did you qualify the client, or were they wasting your time to get a better bid from someone else?

7. Are you using The Quarter Method, or your own version of sales?

I wish you all the best for your future. If you need more training in The Quarter Method, we have national seminars for you to attend, or you can always contact us at TQM Inc. to schedule corporate training: www.thequartermethod. com.

Notes

Notes

Notes

Notes

Look for

THE QUARTER METHOD
Book 2
"Communicating
in High Definition"

Available at Amazon.com
and other booksellers
in late 2015